# Possibilities

Inger Marie Nordin

# Delight

A child knows how to delight
His whole face lights up
like a sunrise
Often followed by
a peal of laughter
as contagious
as chickenpox
You just cannot help
but smile and rejoice
together with the child

# Possibilities

Photographs including cover photo by Inger Marie Nordin
Published by Inger Marie Nordin



ISBN: 978-82-692028-5-4

It does not always take so much
It can be a butterfly
or a tickling finger
or a playful kitten
or a leaping frog
There is so much to delight in
Delight is a bubbling joy
There is no room in our bodies
It must come out

What if we all could delight
in that way
Delight in the small things
delight in the big things
Be on the lookout
for something to delight in
Not finding anything to complain about
or getting irritated about
Figure how many stiff muscles
we could have been spared
How many arguments and sleepless nights
Let yourself delight, let yourself be enthused
Let the child in you take you along
on a journey where anything is possible

# It is in the Air

It is in the air
You have already noticed it
When you rose today
something deep inside
some starting bubbles
Something is afoot

You do not know exactly what it is
It is like you have it
on the tip of your tongue
You notice the taste
Something is on its way

You walk out and turn up your face
You can barely stand still
Your feet are doing a little dance
You just know
Something is about to happen

You are nearly taking off as you walk
Your heart is a balloon
that wants to soar to heaven
Your smile comes from deep within
and has no intention to disappear
You only know
Something is on its way

# Threefold

One can easily break
When the storm is raging
When the blizzard is blazing
When everybody around you is nagging

It is good to be two
It is good to have support
Someone to help and comfort you
When you are getting a big scolding

Three is even better
They stand at your side
When the storms in your life come blazing
You are getting your strength from them

# Roots

A tree was standing so proud and straight
It reached high above the neighbors
But something happened
a wind so sudden and strong
took hold of the vastness of the tree
Suddenly the tree was down and out
What was the cause of the fall
Surely the tree had big roots
Was it rooted deep enough
Obviously not
The roots were shallow
When the wind came
the tree had no chance to resist

Deep roots – a lesson for everybody
Maybe the soil was watered down
empty of nourishment
It had stopped being the good soil
And the tree had no choice
it had no way of moving
But what about me
I really have a choice

A tree can be exposed to wild forces
Survive top breakages and thunderbolts
They can thrive and live for many years
Marked – but in great shape
This was possible
because the roots were strong
The nutrients were exactly right

I too need deep roots
I need to find out what kind of soil
is best for me
So that I will not tumble
when the harsh winds of life
Will try to take me down

# Moss-covered

A mossy stone gives a soft impression
of a blanket of thick, green moss
You want to stroke that velvety blanket
But you know that if you sit down in the softness
you will get thoroughly wet

Next stone seems at a cursory look somewhat better
But at a closer look, you see that this stone
is terribly gnarled
It stings even here and there
It does not invite to closer relationship
for that it is too angular

A little despondently we walk on and find the perfect stone
This smooth, good stone that is calling on you
to sit down and rest your weary legs
It has a perfect shape and adequate height and it lets you relax
and enjoy this great view over the mirrorlike lake

Humans are somewhat like these stones

The mossy can seem to be a good person to be with
But is somewhat difficult to get to know
A little bit woolly at the edges and you do not feel well
after being together with that person

Then there are these that have the perfect shape, at a distance
They can shine and be admired, but in a closer relationship
they become totally intolerable to be with
Their sharp edges can give lasting wounds

Then there are those that by just being there
radiate peace and calm
It is like coming into a peaceful harbor
After a tough sailing where everything has gone wrong
What a good anchoring place

There are many kinds of stones and many kinds of people
But stones can get chipped and honed and it is said
That a man sharpens the countenance of his friend
And the stone you passed last time may have gone through
a transformation in the hands of a master

# Focus

It is time to change focus
Time to direct your sharpness at something else
Your eye and mind can get rest
from the usual settings
what they were used to focus on
namely work in all its kinds
It has been exciting

But
New challenges are waiting
Maybe some extreme close-ups
maybe focus on the things closer to home
that you did not have time for
that you just had to let wait
Maybe open for wide scope
see the big and wide perspective
Discover the joy in new challenges
or go deeper in what you already know
New seasons
New challenges
New joy

# Graining

Graining discloses the life of a tree
The slim, the fat
the light, the dark
Everything is etched
and may be observed
when the life of the tree is over

How would we have looked
What does our graining look like
We have certainly had meagre years
Sometimes because of lack of money
other times because of lack
of strength and courage

Sometimes there were fat years
We had a lot to give in many ways
Sure, there has been times of joy
times when everything was light and easy
Everything was possible and life was a breeze

The dark ones have also been there
The tough where everything was heavy
It was as if you could not breathe
because of weight
or too much speed

How has your tree turned out
It is probably not like mine
There is still time for growth
There is still time for changes

# To Give and Receive

It is a joy to receive
to share with others
to choose the right present to give
A joy to deliver good words
a pat and a hug
to a colleague or brother
It feels good

What about receiving
Is it easy to receive
A wrapped-up gift
is a joy to unwrap
What about praise given to us
That is not as easy
We are lost for words
We want to hide
to look down or to the side
Want to make the words smaller
How is that

Are words more direct
Are words more difficult to receive
Why does it feel undeserved
when the person who says means it
Do we belittle ourselves
What we are doing is good
We just blow it away
and we think, that was not much

We ought to learn to say thank you
To receive praise with an open mind
Come and receive
Lift your eyes
Say thanks with a smile

# To Catch an Instant

A sunbeam brushes a dew drop
A spider web is filled with diamonds
A breeze lifts a leaf
The wind swirls the leaf in a dance

A smile is cautiously sneaking
into the corner of the mouth
A twinkle in his eye comes
as sudden as a summer rain shower

The moment is there
Ready to be caught
by a keen eye that sees it
prepared in thoughts and mind

If it is the lens of the eye
or the photo camera
The joy in the little is just as big
and remains much longer than an instant

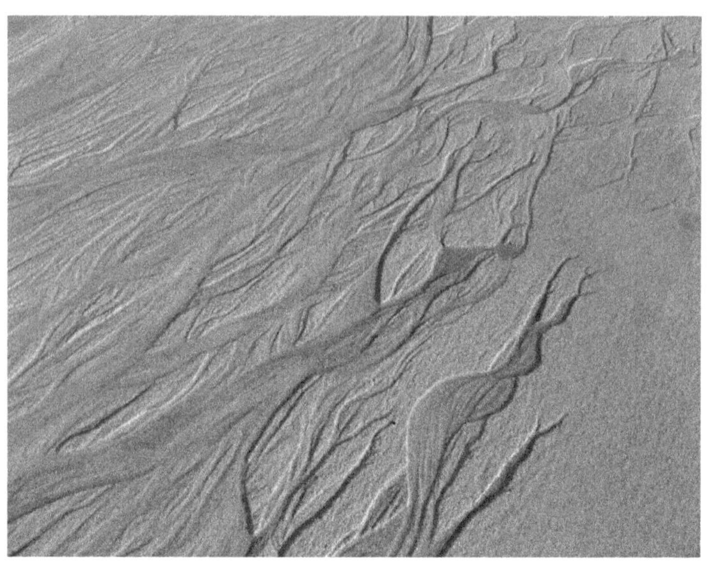

# Traces

*Soft snow*
I remember my wonder
and excitement as a child
as I followed mouse tracks and hare tracks
on mountain trips at Easter
I remember traces of wings from capercaillie
An adventure to a little girl who hoped
that the fox was cheated out of a catch

*Traces in the sand*
A lovely walk a silent summer evening
The waves are washing away the traces
as you walk
It is as if you never were there

*Traces in the face*
Grandma fascinated me
with her many wrinkles
Some of them were laugh lines
while others were chiseled
from the shifting winds of life
easily seen by others

*Invisible traces*
Words leave traces
They are not always visible
A kind glance and a smile
may be the balm
that a heart needs to be healed
While a harsh word can be like a knife
that is opening a newly mended cut

We have all inner traces
Some deeper than others
The traces are a part of us
They are a part of shaping us

Sometimes in close friends' gatherings
We can show the traces
And like an old record
be played to their enjoyment
who appreciate music of the heart

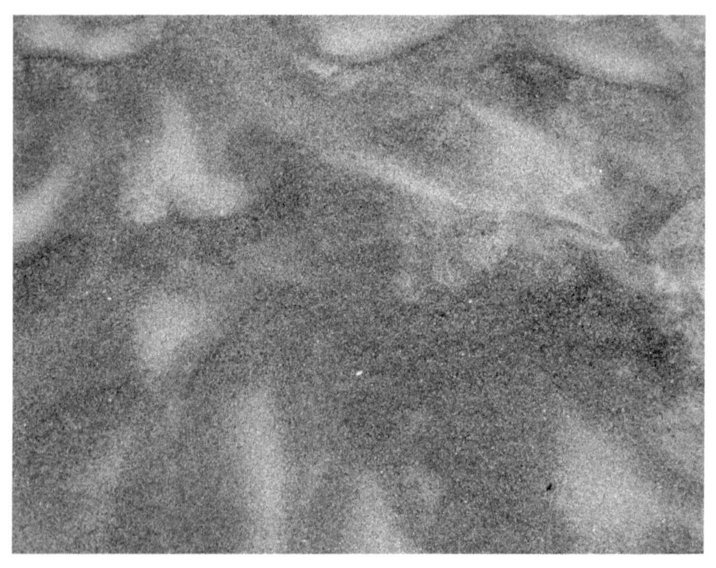

# Words About Words

Good words you have received
may be carried as beautiful pearls
They make you straighten your back
give you a spring in your steps
and a twinkle in your eye

Another word can be one you do not like
a grain of truth
It irritates
But like the sand grain in the oyster
it is covered by layers of mother of pearl
and becomes the most beautiful pearl at last

Words can make you warm
Words can make you cold
They can build or tear down
Sometimes they are empty
and totally void meaning

Sometimes one word is enough
They do not need to come in bunches
Sometimes you need more
some words of explanation
Why everybody else is laughing

Few or many
great or small
Words are important
They remain when we have left

# Some

Some are thinking
Life is good
Life is wonderful
So much good
they have been given

Some are thinking
Life is grey
Life is dreary
Everything is so insignificant

Some are thinking
I am only ridiculed
Life is difficult
Everything feels raw

Some are thinking
of the life they have been given
They are taking everything in their stride
if things happen suddenly

Some are thinking
on big or minor issues
rejoicing over little
over the life they have been given

Some are thinking
Everything happens so fast
Time is too short
Time has passed them by

Some are thinking
That the life they have been given
Is a gift from our Lord
It can be jolly good

# Clean Slate

Clean slates do not come by themselves
They must be chosen
We must decide that enough is enough
and then start afresh

It is not easy
Our thoughts are easily caught in the old
It is like the tongue that often
must touch the old, damaged tooth

Our minds are easily led by old patterns
They are like rails we cannot come out of
And if we try, we easily fall on our faces
but we cannot let that stop us

We need clean slates
We need a new start
It may be in the smaller or greater areas in our lives
And we who see the clean slate
We can provide the crayons

## Change

Changing cloud cover
High pressure, low pressure
The weather is always changing

The wind blows where it wishes
It has the seasons on its back
It carries the promise of sun and warmth
frost and snow

If there is something that is certain
that is that the weather
and the seasons are changing
We are used to it
Maybe it is because of that

we do not like other changes
The weather is enough for us
the challenges that follow
The weather is unpersonal
even if sometimes it does not feel like that

Changes make some of us unsafe
and make us as prickly as a hedgehog
We isolate ourselves

Life is like a river
Sometimes it is slow
Sometimes it is quick
forever changing
If we are going to stay afloat
we cannot become small and dense like a bowl
We must stretch
and make a big surface
Use the strength
the traits we have been given as gifts
Give ourselves good growth conditions
Then we may experience
we have more to go on
It will be easier for us
To stretch a hand
either to give or receive support
in a world that is constantly changing

# Fresh Start

Imagine having a fresh start
Forget what is behind
of lost opportunities
wrong choices
angry words
old prejudices
Words never spoken

Now you and I can start afresh
We can stretch out
and take hold of what is in front of us
Use the possibilities
and the gifts we have received
Dare to walk on water
Dare to say those words
we know we should have said
Just let them come out

Do not let anything stop you
Make a choice and run the race
Do not let self-contempt eat you up
Better to let courage fill you
as you dare to take the first step
One small step into a world
filled with all the possibilities
you can only imagine

## Possibilities

A gate is closing
Impossible to go back
Your thoughts are taking the fast track
They want to linger in the past
Not possible
Hesitantly the first step is taken
Your eyes are glued to the ground
You do not dare to lose your grip
Afraid to fall
Eventually you are more secure
Still your eyes are downcast

A sound makes you stop
You become curious
Suddenly your eyes are lifted
You take some steps
You are taking a turn
The landscape is opening up
You see possibilities
Some simple
Some somewhat difficult
Some impossible
Do not go there

There are always new paths
It takes courage to try
You can take one step
Then another
Before you know it
A new path has been made
You have found your own opportunity

# A Journey

I stand and look back
Many memories
Big, small
Laughter, tears
Fragrance, thoughts
Cozy, precious
Some sorted
Some waiting for the archives
The sore ones still need to be processed
may be seen in a new perspective
The grey ones may suddenly shine
The strong lose some of their glory

I stand and look forward
New memories are waiting
New territories to conquer
The experiences I have in my backpack
may help me in the next season
The bad ones I let go of
They impact me
but do not define who I am
There are a lot of good things waiting for me
Excitement
Discoveries
Joy
Challenges
Some rain showers as well
I am shod for them
Time to go

# The Story

It is a new season
A new page in the book
You turn a page
eagerly waiting
what is to come
The book has been exciting so far
You have enjoyed the story
You are looking forward to the continuation

When you have turned the page
You notice there are many empty lines in between
Your story has not been written yet
Some things are set
You must fill out the rest
That is your mission
your life
I am sure it is going to be
an exciting book
we all are going to want to read

# The Joy of Choosing

Think about choosing
Not to be closed and locked
to sit down and think
let time be an advisor
to enjoy choosing
take another path
something totally unexpected
to take a side road
that was a little rough to walk

To search your capabilities
you only felt were there
To use other colors
you did not think were quite you
They make you smile
and others to wonder

Choices can be big
Choices can be small
Do not let the fear decide
Some rapid heart beats
can be a companion for your choice
It takes courage to chose
Retrieve your courage
Find your joy in choosing
Let the doubt sail off on its way

## Spring Visit

The sun is on a visit through my window
It comes like a spotlight
and draws a square on the floor
My cat discovers it at once
And curls up in pure delight
because of the lovely warmth

The cat slaps lazily a wintered fly
that suddenly awakens
The sunbeams are waltzing with the dust
and play hide and seek with some dust bunnies
who in vain try to hide under the sofa

I am shutting my eyes
and refuse to look at the stripes on my windows
I am doing like the cat
enjoying myself in the warmth of the spring sun
and thinking: Welcome back
Let there be light!

# A Hot Spring Day

The breakers are dashing lazily
inwards the beach
They have lost their energy
and are only playing a bit
with a small piece of wood
Lying on the water surface

The breakers make a little more effort
and wash in a bobbly way
away some footprints
that have been left alone
Now they are gone

The breakers retire
The sun is reflected in the sand
before the breakers come again
and play hide and seek with the beams
A slow and lazy game

# The Wind

The wind is playing in the dry grass
It is swirling up old dust and leaves
that had descended like a blanket over all
We got used to that
Now the wind is lifting them and sending them away
Now we can see the green sprouts waiting

It was not lifeless
It was only hidden
Dust and leaves were only a covering

What if we have such a covering
If there was a fresh wind that came
and blew away everything old
Old thoughts
Old patterns
Old clutter
What if the new
was allowed to come up
Got life and light

Come all winds
Come and blow on me
I need light and life
Come all winds
blow away all the spider webs
that are sitting like glue
over all the fresh thoughts
Blow away heavy thoughts
those that are saying
that I cannot or will not be able to
I can and I will
Come my own wind
I am ready
It is time

## Summer Morning

Dewy grass
The sun is creating diamonds of dew drops
The spider web becomes a glistening work of art
The flowers are opening up and is greeting the sun
as it is touching the petals

The butterfly is dancing
as it is flitting from flower to flower
The bumble bee is murmuring good-naturedly in tune
as it is humming away

The hover fly is skipping jerkily
The birds are having their morning concert
attuned as a choir

It is early
It is too early

# Summer Memories

Summer
A word filled with taste, flavor and sound
The taste of strawberry and ice cream
The taste of crispy trout
caught in a mountain lake
mirrorlike and quiet

The whiff of newly cut hay
The whiff of salty water
as you stroll along a beach with bare toes
You are feeling the calmness coming
You can breathe oh so deeply

The sound of jubilant larks
playing high up in the sky
The sound of buzzing bees
The sound of splashing children
enjoying themselves immensely

Draw your breath deeply
Close your eyes
Let your thoughts linger
with good summer memories
Let the taste, smell and sound
fill you with joy and peace

Let this summer
bring lasting memories
not of stress and whining
but of joy and wonder
Let the child in you have plenty of room
to rejoice and be happy
about the summer's many wonders

# Shift

Quiet, so quiet
A shift
almost unnoticed
but it is there
The flower hanging with its head
straightens up in position
It is preparing for the worst
that is coming

The wind is sending a vanguard
that is a warning about gusts to come
Then it comes in a rush
and is ruffling the hairstyle of the trees
The leaves are rattling in protest
No one is listening

The clouds are not let alone
They are pushed on
They are travelling by express speed
until the steam is out
and heaven and earth can breathe again
The leaves are calming down
and the flower can get a nap

# Wind Ruff

A summer breeze is ruffling my hair
It wants to play
as if it wants to tease me a bit
It is time to be playful
Forget the serious thoughts
Let go of self-importance

A wind is puffing around the corner
It surprises you
You thought you had everything in order
Every thought in neat rows

The wind gets you unbalanced
You must renew your mind
Make new thought patterns

An autumn storm is tearing and ruffling
An unbending mind
has difficulties with resisting
Their stances are torn down
They either are crushed
or are completely changing directions

The wind is taking hold of a sail
It is filling the sail
And the ship is picking up speed

Are you lifting your sail
Do you let the wind
fill the sails of your own thoughts
so that you can speed along
in new power and strength
If you do not
you may get into the backwaters

The wind is blowing wherever it wants
Are you coming?

## Harvest

Autumn
A dark and wet season
for some
A valuable season
for some
A time of stillness and reflection
for some

For others
a busy season
The season of harvesting
Things you have tended and watered

cropped or sown
are to be harvested
Time for truth
What was the result

What have we been sowing
Because everybody has sown
Plants, words or deeds
We sow every day
What do we sow
Smiles
Anger
Laughter
Scolding
Encouragement
Contempt
Comfort

We are reaping what we have been sowing
So, it says
Sometimes it does not seem so
The smile we are giving
Is getting us a pout as an answer
The encouragement we are bringing
is getting us a scowling look

But
Who knows what is happening inside
Maybe the permafrost
inside the heart
is about to thaw
and you were a part
to start the whole thing

## Revisited

The wind is blowing, and the leaves are dancing
before they are settling down like a soft blanket
on the stony road

That road you have walked so many times
There you have shed your brave tears
That road that has listened to your dreams and cries

Now there are new memories and new thoughts
That must be processed
Your feet find their way, you know the way blindfolded
Your smile and the tears come easily
It is good to have known territory under your feet

Your feet are stopping by themselves at an old tree
The tree is furrowed, and weather beaten
and an old friend
You are giving the tree a friendly pat
before you let your thoughts propel you

Just like the thoughts and memories
are swirling inside your head
the wind is making swirls with the leaves
and will not let it lie still

Soon you are at the end of the road
You feel the peace descending
like a duvet over your mind
just as the road is covered by autumn yellow leaves

# Masquerade Ball

The wind is running through the forest
It is taking hold of everything
from the highest top
to the lowest heather
Everything is to be shaken

This summer every leaf was green
Different shapes
but almost the same color
Now the colors are outshining each other
It is as if they finally
can let their masks go
Show who they really are

This is I

Do we have a mask
Do we try to hide who we are
Do we try to be like the others
or are we letting our own colors come forth
beautiful colors in all variations
Together we can make
the most beautiful quilt
as the autumn is making his

# Winter Sun

The sun is looking over the edge of the duvet
Was it morning already
He was inclined to go to sleep again
but duty called

Tentatively he stretched outside the duvet
It was cold
It was frost
The sun nearly regretted not staying in bed

It was beautiful to watch the beams playing
along the sparkling snow
No, he just had to rise

The sun was not going so high up
not now
The light was warm and pink
As the sun entered the sky

The frost looked almost warm
How funny
The sun made itself ready for the ride

He looked forward to the evening
Then the beams would glide
over the sparkling surfaces
and give some color
to the winter dressed landscape

# About the Author

Inger Marie Nordin began her Christian journey at 14 years of age, growing to hear God's voice after being baptized in the Spirit at 16. She moves in the gifts of teaching and prophecy—seeing the supernatural behind the natural—and enjoys ministering at her church, singing in the Spirit and taking photographs of God's creation. Inger began writing poetry as the Lord ministered to her during a difficult time in her life and is now led to pass it on to others. She makes her home in Oslo, Norway, and gives thanks to God for her daughter, son-in-law and two grandsons.

www.ingramcontent.com/pod-product-compliance
Ingram Content Group UK Ltd.
Pitfield, Milton Keynes, MK11 3LW, UK
UKHW062254290726
14090UKWH00017B/691